THE CABOOSE

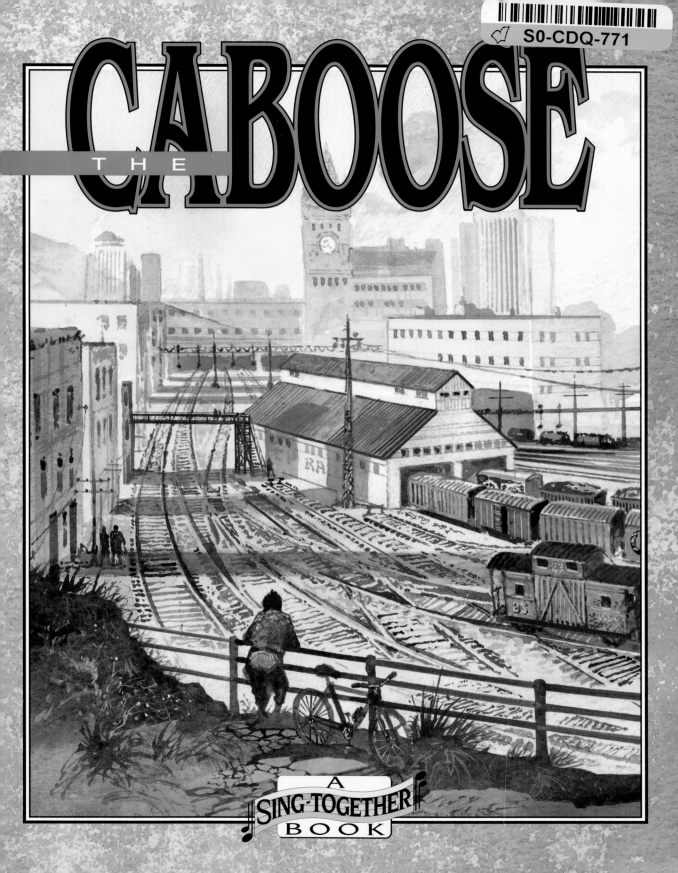

A SING-TOGETHER BOOK

I like to count every car
On every train that passes by.
And on each and every train
There is one car to catch my eye.

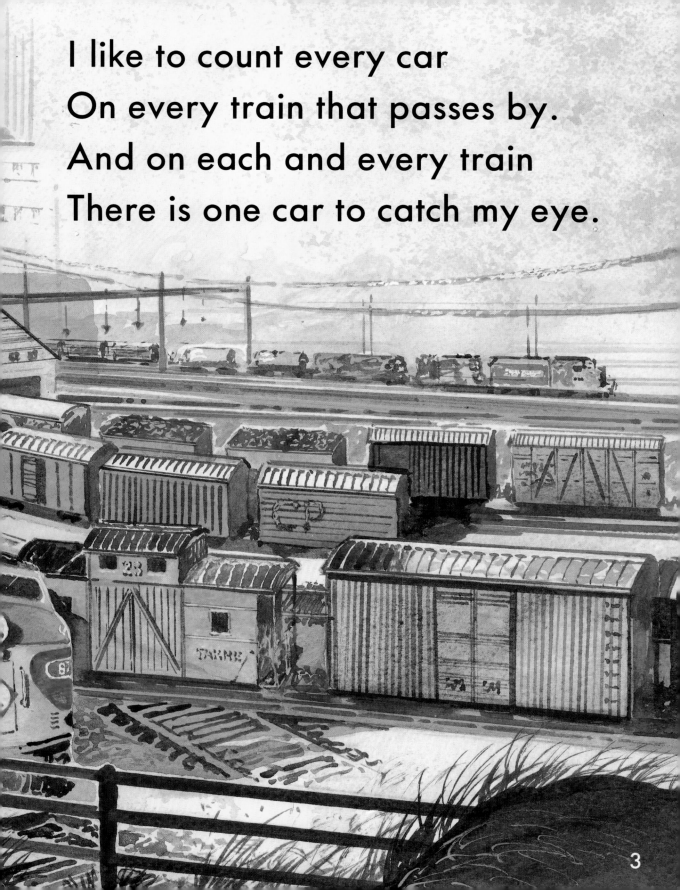

The prettiest car
On the whole train by far
Is the one at the back...
the caboose.

I know the engine is the worker
With her headlight shining bright.
And the passenger
   and freight cars
Carry loads both
   day and night.

But who's bringing up the rear
With the workers and their gear?
The one at the back...
    the caboose.

Not one other car is the same,
No matter how long the train.

Even though it's alone at the back,
It's the prettiest car on the track.

When the trainman
    has to wave a lamp
For other trains to see,
I imagine that it's
    his way
To say good-bye to me.

But I'll see him again
On the very next train.
The one at the back...
    the caboose.

So... if a yellow, red,
or orange caboose
Should ever pass you by,
It might be your last chance
To wave and say good-bye.
Take the opportunity
Before it's just a memory.
The one at the back...
the caboose.

The prettiest car on the track...
the caboose.
Faithful friend at the end...
the caboose.